FABER EARLY ORGAN SERIES

European Organ Music of the 16th & 17th Centuries
Series Editor : James Dalton

Volume 12

The Netherlands & N. Germany

c.1650-c.1710

WECKMANN · BUXTEHUDE
BRUHNS · BÖHM

EDITED BY

HENRIK GLAHN & HAAKON ELMER

WITH AN INTRODUCTION BY

GEOFFREY WEBBER

Faber Music Limited

London

© 1988 by Faber Music Ltd
First published in 1988 by Faber Music Ltd
3 Queen Square London WC1N 3AU
Music engraved by Christopher Hinkins
Typeset by Goodfellow & Egan, Cambridge
Cover and text designed by M & S Tucker
Cover illustration by John Brennan
German translations by Katharina Brett
Printed in England

Access to sources used in the preparation of this volume
was by kind permission of the following libraries: Deutsche
Staatsbibliothek, Berlin: Gemeentemuseum, The Hague;
Musikbibliothek der Stadt, Leipzig; Ratsbücherei,
Lüneburg; Staatsbibliothek Preussischer Kulturbesitz,
Berlin.

The facsimile on page ix is reproduced by permission of the
Staatsbibliothek Preussischer Kulturbesitz.

Most of the selection and editing of the music in this
volume was completed by Henrik Glahn and Haakon
Elmer before the latter's death in February 1984. Since
then Henrik Glahn has been responsible for the edition.

Contents – Inhalt

Editorial Procedure *p. iv*   *Anmerkung des Herausgebers S. vi*
Introduction *p. iv*   *Vorwort S. vii*
Ornamentation *p. v*   *Ornamentierung S. viii*
Registration *p. v*   *Registrierung S. viii*

1 · Gelobet seist du, Jesu Christ   *Matthias Weckmann (c.1619–1674)*   2

2 · Ciacona (in C minor, BuxWV159)   *Dietrich Buxtehude (c.1637–1707)*   15

3 · Mensch, willt du leben seliglich (BuxWV206)   *Dietrich Buxtehude*   21

4 · Praeludium (in E minor)   *Nicolaus Bruhns (1665–1697)*   23

5 · Vater unser im Himmelreich   *Georg Böhm (1661–1733)*   29

6 · Praeludium con Fuga (in A minor)   *Georg Böhm*   32

Critical Commentary *p. 36*

Appendix: Analytical Index to the Faber Early Organ Series *p. 38*

Editorial Procedure

This is a practical performing edition. All the pieces are presented in modern staff notation using treble and bass clefs. Within this arrangement, as much information as possible about the original sources is included on the score – considerably more, in some cases, than is found in other modern editions. The result, however, is not a facsimile in easy clefs; the editorial method that has been evolved is summarised as follows:

1. Unless otherwise indicated, original note-values, bar-lines, key-signatures and time-signatures have been preserved, and the distribution of notes between the staves retained. (In final chords, original note-values have been preserved even where not every part has the same number of beats.) Owing to the use of modern staves and clefs, original stem directions have sometimes been altered, but an attempt has been made to retain the idiomatic free-voiced appearance of the original notation. Pieces notated in open score have been transcribed onto two staves.
2. Original clefs and/or notation are indicated at the beginning of each piece, and at other points where necessary. Where a time-signature or proportion-sign occurring in the course of a piece has been altered, the original is shown between the staves.
3. Where unusual notation (e.g. black semibreves, white demi-semi-minims) appears in the original, it has been changed to a modern equivalent and noted in the Commentary.
4. Note-values extending over bar-lines have been transcribed using ties; otherwise, original note-groupings (unconventional beaming of quavers included) have been preserved. Although this can produce the appearance of inconsistency, there is often a purpose to the original script, and alteration in some cases but not in others would produce a confused picture.
5. Accidentals have been reproduced in full as they occur in the sources, except that, where applicable, sharps and flats have been replaced by modern naturals (for example, f♮ is often given as f♭ in the original, and b♮ as b♯). Normally, an original accidental applies only to one note and immediate repetitions of it; where it appears to hold good for longer than this, no editorial marking has been added, and the modern convention of an accidental being effective for the remainder of the bar applies (the same convention applies in the case of accidentals supplied editorially). All editorial accidentals are given at full size in square brackets, except for cancelling accidentals in tablature notation, which are not strictly speaking editorial, since every note has its own symbol; these are therefore left unbracketed. Some editorial accidentals are essential because of the different conventions governing old and modern notation, while others are suggestions; the types can be distinguished by context.
6. Editorial ornaments, notes, rests and other details are given in square brackets. Ties added editorially are shown as ⌢. Editorial bar-lines are left unjoined between the staves, while in the occasional case of re-barring the original bar-lines are given in heavy type above the stave. The interpolation of a longer or shorter bar should not be seen as invalidating the underlying rhythmic flow. Original indications of part-movement have been retained; editorial indications are shown by broken lines.
7. For any piece appearing in more than one source, a main source has been chosen. It appears at the top of the list of sources for that piece in the Commentary, and its text is regarded as basic. Any deviations from it (where, for instance, corrections have been made by the editor or where another source provides a superior reading) are noted in the Commentary. No attempt has been made to provide an exhaustive list of variants in additional sources.
8. A title has been provided at the head of each piece. Where titles and ascriptions are given in the sources, they are noted, in their original spellings, in the Commentary.

Introduction

In the early seventeenth century north German organ music had owed much to the teaching of Sweelinck, but as the century progressed his influence gradually gave way to the increasing supremacy throughout Europe of Italian music. The varied career of Matthias Weckmann (c1619–1674), one of the central figures in the music of north Germany around the mid-century, may serve to illustrate this transition. In his childhood years in Dresden, Weckmann sang as a chorister under Heinrich Schütz, one of the first composers (and certainly the finest) to relate the new Italian style to German music. Showing promise as an organist, in 1633 Weckmann was sent by Schütz to study at Hamburg, then the main north German centre of organ music. There he studied with the former Sweelinck pupil Jacob Praetorius, organist of the Jacobikirche, and would also have come into contact with other famous organists such as Heinrich Scheidemann.

Weckmann returned to Dresden in 1637 as organist of the electoral chapel, where he was in close contact with the numerous Italian musicians employed at the court, and also took part in a keyboard playing competition with the visiting south German organist Johann Jacob Froberger (1616–1667), with whom he was to remain a lifelong friend. Weckmann's continued association with Schütz led to a spell of a few years at the Danish court, but he did not leave his Dresden post until 1655, when he returned to Hamburg to become organist of the Jacobikirche. A few years later he founded a Collegium Musicum,[1] a society of musicians and music-lovers who met to provide weekly concerts in the refectory of the cathedral. With a keen eye on the most recent developments in music, the society performed works from Venice, Rome, Vienna, Munich and other major centres. Thus Weckmann had links both with the early seventeenth-century north German organists and with the new interest in Italian music, and both influences may be observed in his surviving music.

In his free organ works and vocal music, Weckmann stands out as one of the most Italianate German composers of his generation, but in his chorale settings he stays close to the heritage of Sweelinck. His four-verse setting of *Gelobet seist du, Jesu Christ* (No. 1) belongs to the Lutheran liturgical tradition, where sung chorales were often interspersed with solo verses improvised by the organist (see Introduction to Vol. 11). In this particular work verse 2 stands out as a chorale fantasia within a set of simpler variations. Features recalling earlier organ music include the use of echo effects in this verse, and runs in parallel thirds and sixths in verse 4.

In contrast, Buxtehude's setting of *Mensch, willt du leben seliglich* (No. 3) illustrates how in the later seventeenth century composers were abandoning patterned figuration in favour of spontaneous and rhetorical gestures, seen here in the embellishments to the chorale melody. However, the accompaniment uses a typical contrapuntal texture, unlike that of *Vater unser im Himmelreich* (No. 5) by Georg Böhm (1661–1733), organist of the Johanniskirche in Lüneburg from 1698. Here the continuous repeated-note accompaniment is reminiscent of Italian string music, while the extravagant Baroque ornamentation that saturates the *cantus firmus* is an outstanding example of the influence of contemporary French keyboard music on north German composers.

The use of ostinato basses was a favourite technique of seventeenth-century Italian composers, and the north Germans also made excellent use of this practice. Several examples appear in the vocal and chamber music of Weckmann, Buxtehude and others, and Buxtehude wrote three ostinato pieces for organ (two chaconnes and a passacaglia) and included ostinato sections in three of his *praeludia*. The C minor *Ciacona* (No. 2) is rich in both figuration and harmony, and it is striking that the theme proper is almost completely abandoned after bar 41, only its harmonic framework being retained. Material characteristic of Buxtehude, such as the rhetorical rests towards the end and the semiquaver figuration from bar 53, appears alongside techniques familiar from other German keyboard chaconnes, such as those of Johann Caspar Kerll and Johann Pachelbel, including dotted rhythms and the *arpeggiando*, or *séparé*, style.

The *praeludium* was the chief area of change and development in north German organ music of the late seventeenth century, reflecting an increasing interest in organ music outside the immediate requirements of the liturgy. In contrast to the pattern of prelude and fugue familiar in Bach's mature organ works, the structure of the earlier *praeludium* was far from standardised. Its structural model was the Italian variation canzona, where a number of fugal sections based on variants of the same theme were often linked by short free sections. The young Nicolaus Bruhns (1665–1697) was fortunate in being a pupil of Buxtehude, the leading exponent of the *praeludium* (see Vol. 11, No. 7), and the

opening pedal flourish of his *Praeludium* in E minor (No. 4) was probably one of a number of techniques he learned from his teacher. Though this work contains only a single fugal section, traces of the variation canzona are evident both in the multisectional structure and also in the thematic link between the fugue and the *Allegro* beginning at bar 89. The fugal subject is strikingly similar to the Corelli theme (from his Op. 3 trio sonatas of 1689) used by J. S. Bach in his Fugue in B minor BWV579, and the fact that Bruhns was a virtuoso violinist as well as organist would help to explain his familiarity with the Italian string style.

The *Praeludium con Fuga* (No. 6) by Böhm also betrays a knowledge of contemporary Italian string music, in its semiquaver figuration and in the sequential harmony that dominates the fugue from bar 53. The repeated notes and rests in the fugue subject are typical of late seventeenth-century north German style, but in its overall structure the work is one of the earliest manifestations of the trend towards the bipartite prelude and fugue of the eighteenth century.

1 See M. Seiffert: 'Matthias Weckmann und das Collegium Musicum in Hamburg', *Sammelbände der internationalen Musik-Gesellschaft*, ii (1900–1901), p. 76

Ornamentation

During the latter part of the seventeenth century the style of ornamentation outlined in Vols. 10 and 11 of this anthology – basically that of the Renaissance – gave way to the Baroque style characteristic of the French *clavecinistes*. The essential new elements of this style were the increased use of the appoggiatura, both on its own and as a prefix to trills and mordents, and a certain rhythmic flexibility in the performance of ornaments.

Böhm's *Vater unser* (no. 5) is one of the most elaborate examples of the use of the new style by German organists around the turn of the eighteenth century, and presents something of a challenge to the player. The accompaniment provides a regular rhythmic pulse, while the *cantus firmus* line requires considerable freedom of expression, especially where extra small notes are used. The sign ⟋ indicates a *tremblement*, or trill beginning on the upper auxiliary, with the number of repercussions varying according to context. In places where the upper-note start impairs the melodic line (e.g. bars 31–3) a *tremblement lié*, in which the upper auxiliary

is tied over from the preceding melody note, would be more appropriate. The sign ⟋ indicates the *pincé* or mordent, a quick alternation of the main note and the lower auxiliary. The *Schleifer* or slide, is indicated by the sign ⟋ . French authorities describe this as beginning on the beat ⟋ but some German sources[2] suggest a realization before the beat. The placing of small grace notes before the beat seems likely in bars 16, 28 and 36, though in bars 5 and 10, where they follow a rest, it may seem more appropriate to play them on the beat.

The other pieces in this volume contain no signs for ornamentation but, as in the earlier repertoire, the skilled player should feel free to add ornaments discreetly and in an appropriate style.

2 E.g. J. G. Walther: *Praecepta der musicalischen Composition* (Leipzig, 1708), and a setting by Bruhns of *Nun komm, der Heiden Heiland*, which has written-out slides before the beat.

Registration

Many north German organs built or enlarged during the seventeenth century were of considerable size, offering countless possibilities for the solo and accompaniment combinations required for the performance of chorale settings, and a number of contrasting *pleni* for the performance of free works. The Pedal departments were among the largest in Europe. Buxtehude had two organs in the Lübeck Marienkirche, the smaller of which, the 'Totentanzorgel', was a three-manual instrument with pedals, while the organ at the west end had the following specification during Buxtehude's time:[3]

Werk		*Rückpositiv*	
Principal	16'	Principal	8'
Quintadena	16'	Bordun	16'
Octava	8'	Blockflöte	8'
Spitz-Flöte	8'	Sesquialtera	II
Octava	4'	Hohl-Flöte	8'

(*Werk*)		(*Rückpositiv*)	
Hohlflöte	4'	Quintadena	8'
Nasat	3' [=2⅔']	Octava	4'
Rauschpfeiffe	IV	Spiel-Flöte	2'
Scharff	IV	Mixtura	V
Mixtura	XV	Dulcian	16'
Trommete	16'	Baarpfeiffe	8'
Trommete	8'	Trichter-Regal	8'
Zinke	8'	Vox humana	8'
		Scharff	IV–V
Brust			
Principal	8'	*Pedal*	
Gedact	8'	Principal	32'
Octava	4'	Sub-Bass	16'
Hohlflöte	4'	Octava	8'
Sesquialtera	II	Bauerflöte	2'
Feld-Pfeiffe	2'	Mixtura	VI

(Brust)		(Pedal)	
Gemshorn	2'	Gross-Posaun (from F?)	32'
Sifflet	1½'	Posaune	16'
Mixtura	VIII	Trommete	8'
Cimbel	III	Principal	16'
Krumhorn	8'	Gedact	8'
Regal	8'	Octava	4'
		Nachthorn	2'
Cimbel-Stern; 2 drums		Dulcian	16'
('Trummeln'); 2 tremulants		Krumhorn	8'
[Couplers]		Cornet	2'

In an account of Matthias Weckmann's audition at the Hamburg Jacobikirche given by his pupil Johann Kortkamp,[4] it is recorded that at one point Weckmann used a favourite chorale registration of his former teacher Jacob Praetorius, which consisted of the following: Oberwerk Trommete 8', Zinke 8', Nassat 2', Gemsshorn 2', Hohlfleute 4'; Rückpositiv Prinzipal 8', Octave 4' (for the quieter middle voices), Pedal Posaune 16', Trommete 8' and 4', Cornet 2'.[5] It is interesting to note the use of solo stops on both the Oberwerk and Pedal, the particular combination of reed, flute and mutation stops used on the Oberwerk, and the unusual use of the Rückpositiv for the accompanying voices. Such a combination may well be suitable for verse 2 of Weckmann's *Gelobet seist du*

(No. 1) where the chorale melody is heard both in the upper voice and in the pedal. However, from the manual indications in the source it would seem that the roles of Rückpositiv and Oberwerk should be reversed, so that the Rückpositiv fulfils its traditional function of bearing the melody.

The indications for registration given by Böhm at the start of his *Vater unser* (No. 5) suggest the use of some Principal tone in the Pedal, flutes for the Oberwerk and solo stops for the Rückpositiv, probably using either a solo reed such as a Regal or Krummhorn, or a Sesquialtera combination.

Few clues survive as to the registration of works in free style, but given their sectional nature, and considering the intricate manual changes indicated in some chorale settings, it seems likely that changes of manual would be appropriate between sections.

Geoffrey Webber
Oxford, 1987

3 From F. E. Niedt, *Musicalische Handleitung* (Hamburg, 1721, repr. by Frits Knuf B.V.: The Netherlands, 1976), p. 189. See also K. J. Snyder, 'Buxtehude's Organs: Helsingor, Helsingborg, Lübeck 2: The Lübeck Organs', *The Musical Times*, cxxvi (1985), p. 429
4 See J. T. Kite-Powell: *The Visby (Petri) Organ Tablature: Investigation and Critical Edition*, Quellen-Kataloge zur Musikgeschichte, xix (Wilhelmshaven: Heinrichshofen, 1979)
5 The specification of the Jacobikirche organ is given in Vol. 11.

Anmerkung des Herausgebers

Die vorliegende Ausgabe richtet sich an praktizierende Musiker. Alle Musikstücke erscheinen in moderner Liniennotation unter Verwendung von Violin- und Baßschlüsseln. Die Partituren dieser Ausgabe enthalten so viel Information wie möglich über die Originalquellen – in einigen Fällen bedeutend mehr, als in anderen modernen Ausgaben zu finden ist. Das Resultat ist jedoch nicht eine vereinfachte Reproduktion des Originals. Eine systematische Methode der Herausgabe wurde entwickelt, die im Folgenden zusammengefaßt wird:

1. Wenn nicht anders vermerkt, sind die Notenwerte, Taktstriche, Tonart und Taktvorzeichen des Originals beibehalten worden, ebenso die Verteilung der Noten auf die einzelnen Systeme. (In Schlußakkorden sind die Notenwerte des Originals beibehalten worden, auch da, wo nicht jede Stimme die gleiche Anzahl Schläge zählt.) Wegen der neuzeitlichen Notenlinien und -schlüssel ist die Richtung der Notenhälse manchmal geändert worden, doch hat man versucht, die idiomatische freie Notation des Originals beizubehalten. Mehrstimmige Partituren sind auf zwei Systeme umgeschrieben worden.

2. Die Original-Notenschlüssel und/oder -Notationen sind am Anfang von jedem Stück vermerkt, und auch anderswo, wenn nötig. Wo ein Taktvorzeichen oder eine Mensuralnotation mitten im Stück abgeändert worden ist, erscheint das Originalzeichen zwischen den Systemen.

3. Wo im Original eine ungewöhnliche Notation auftritt (z.B. schwarze ganze Noten, weiße Achtelnoten) ist die entsprechende moderne Notation verwendet und im kritischen Kommentar erwähnt worden.

4. Notenwerte, die sich über Taktstriche hinaus erstrecken, sind umgeschrieben worden unter der Verwendung von Haltebögen; im übrigen sind die Notengruppierungen des Originals (einschließlich unkonventionellen Verbindens von Achtelnoten mit Balken) beibehalten worden. Trotz dieser scheinbaren Inkonsequenz ist die Originalnotation nicht unbegründet, und eine Abänderung würde in gewissen, wenn auch nicht in allen Fällen zur Verwirrung führen.

5. In den Quellen enthaltene Vorzeichen sind unverändert übernommen worden, mit der Ausnahme, daß allfällige Erhöhungs- und Erniedrigungszeichen durch moderne Notation ersetzt worden

sind (z.B. f♮ erscheint im Original oft als f♭, und e♮ als e♯). Normalerweise gilt ein Vorzeichen im Original nur für eine Note und gleich darauf folgende Wiederholungen; wo es länger zu gelten scheint, gilt ohne Vermerk des Herausgebers die heutige Konvention, wonach ein Vorzeichen für den Rest des Taktes in Kraft bleibt. (Die gleiche Regel gilt für Vorzeichen, die vom Herausgeber hinzugefügt wurden.) Alle Vorzeichen des Herausgebers sind in voller Größe in eckigen Klammern gegeben, mit der Ausnahme von aufgehobenen Vorzeichen in Tabulaturnotation, die genau genommen nicht Hinzufügungen des Herausgebers sind, da jede Note ihr eigenes Symbol hat. Einige vom Herausgeber hinzugefügte Vorzeichen sind unumgänglich infolge der verschiedenen Konventionen der alten und modernen Notation, während andere als Anregungen betrachtet werden sollten. Die zwei Arten sind aus dem Zusammenhang ersichtlich.

6. Vom Herausgeber hinzugefügte Verzierungen, Noten, Pausen und andere Einzelheiten befinden sich in eckigen Klammern. Vom Herausgeber beigefügte Haltebögen erscheinen wie folgt: ⌢. Taktstriche des Herausgebers sind zwischen den Systemen unverbunden, während bei gelegentlichem neuen Einsetzen von Taktstrichen die Originaltaktstriche in Fettdruck über den Systemen erscheinen. Das Einsetzen eines längeren oder kürzeren Taktes hat nicht die Absicht, den zugrunde liegenden rhythmischen Ablauf zu verändern. Hinweise auf den Verlauf der Stimmen im Original sind beibehalten worden; Zusätze des Herausgebers verwenden gestrichelte Linien.

7. Für jedes Werk, das in mehr als einer Quelle erscheint, wurde eine Hauptquelle gewählt. Sie erscheint am Anfang der Liste der Quellen für das betreffende Stück im kritischen Kommentar, und diese Version wird als Grundlage betrachtet. Allfällige Abweichungen von der Hauptquelle (z.B. wo vom Herausgeber Korrekturen angebracht wurden oder wo stellenweise eine andere Quelle vorgezogen wurde) sind im Kommentar vermerkt. Wir haben keinen Versuch unternommen, eine erschöpfende Liste von Varianten in anderen Quellen zu erstellen.

8. Jedes Werk ist mit einer Überschrift versehen worden. Wo Überschriften und Zuschreibungen in den Quellen enthalten sind, sind sie in der Schreibweise des Originals im Kommentar erwähnt.

Vorwort

Die norddeutsche Orgelmusik des frühen 17. Jahrhunderts verdankte vieles der Schule von Sweelinck, aber im Laufe des Jahrhunderts wich Sweelincks Einfluss allmählich zurück, hauptsächlich wegen der zunehmenden Vorrangstellung der italienischen Musik in ganz Europa. Die abwechslungsreiche Laufbahn von Matthias Weckmann (ca.1619–1674), eine der bedeutendsten Persönlichkeiten in der norddeutschen Musik um die Mitte des Jahrhunderts, liefert ein Beispiel für diesen Übergang. Als Kind in Dresden war Weckmann Chorknabe unter Heinrich Schütz, einem der ersten Komponisten, welche den neuen italienischen Stil der deutschen Musik anpassten, und sicher der beste unter ihnen. Weckmann zeigte sich als begabter Orgelschüler und wurde 1633 von Schütz zum Studium nach Hamburg geschickt, damals Norddeutschlands führendes Zentrum der Orgelmusik. Er studierte dort bei einem ehemaligen Sweelinck-Schüler, Jacob Praetorius, dem Organisten der Jacobikirche, und kam wahrscheinlich auch mit anderen berühmten Organisten, wie z.B. Heinrich Scheidemann, in Kontakt.

Weckmann kehrte 1637 als Organist der kurfürstlichen Kapelle nach Dresden zurück und stand dort in engem Kontakt mit den zahlreichen italienischen Musikern, die am Hof angestellt waren. Er beteiligte sich auch an einem Klavierwettstreit mit dem süddeutschen Organisten Johann Jacob Froberger (1616–1667), und die beiden wurden Freunde fürs Leben. Weckmanns Beziehung zu Schütz führte zu einem Aufenthalt von einigen Jahren am dänischen Hof, aber er gab seine Dresdner Stelle erst 1655 auf, als er nach Hamburg zurückkehrte, um Organist der Jacobikirche zu werden. Einige Jahre später gründete er ein Collegium Musicum,[1] einen Verein von Musikern und Musikfreunden, welche sich trafen, um wöchentliche Konzerte im Refektorium des Domes zu veranstalten. Der Verein behielt die neuesten Entwicklungen in der Musik ständig im Auge und führte Werke aus Venedig, Rom, Wien, München und anderen wichtigen Zentren auf. Weckmann hatte daher Beziehungen sowohl zu den norddeutschen Organisten des frühen 17. Jahrhunderts als auch zum neuen Stil der italienischen Musik, und beide Einflüsse sind in seinen erhaltenen Werken deutlich erkennbar.

Was seine freien Orgelwerke und seine Vokalmusik betrifft, fällt Weckmann als einer der von der italienischen Schule am stärksten beeinflussten deutschen Komponisten seiner Generation auf; in seinen Choralbearbeitungen jedoch hält er sich dicht an Sweelincks Erbe. Seine vierstrophige Bearbeitung von *Gelobet seist du, Jesu Christ* (Nr. 1) gehört der lutherischen liturgischen Tradition an, in der gesungene Choralstrophen oft mit vom Organisten improvisierten Solostrophen abwechselten (siehe Vorwort zu Band 11). In dem vorliegenden Stück hebt sich die zweite Strophe – eine Choralfantasie – von einer Reihe einfacherer Variationen ab. Zu den Merkmalen, welche an die frühere Orgelmusik erinnern, gehören die Echoeffekte in der 2. Strophe und die Läufe in parallelen Terzen und Sexten in der 4. Strophe.

Im Gegensatz zu diesem Stück zeigt Buxtehudes Bearbeitung von *Mensch, willt du leben seliglich* (Nr. 3), wie die Komponisten im späteren 17. Jahrhundert Figurationsmuster aufgaben, und stattdessen spontane rhetorische Gesten bevorzugten, wie hier die Verzierungen der Choralmelodie. Zur Begleitung benutzt Buxtehude eine typisch kontrapunktische Struktur, ganz anders als die, die im Stück *Vater unser im Himmelreich* (Nr. 5) von Georg Böhm (1661–1733, ab 1698 Organist der Johanniskirche in Lüneburg) vorkommt, wo die fortlaufenden, wiederholten Töne der Begleitung an die italienische Streichmusik erinnern, während

die extravagante barocke Ornamentierung, die den *cantus firmus* durchflutet, ein hervorragendes Beispiel für den Einfluss der zeitgenössischen französischen Tastenmusik auf norddeutsche Komponisten liefert.

Der *basso ostinato* war eine Lieblingstechnik der italienischen Komponisten des 17. Jahrhunderts und wurde auch in Norddeutschland voll ausgenutzt. Es gibt mehrere Beispiele davon in der Vokal- und Kammermusik von Weckmann, Buxtehude und anderen. Buxtehude komponierte auch drei Ostinatostücke für Orgel (zwei Chaconnen und eine Passacaglia), und ausserdem enthälten drei von seinen *Praeludien* Ostinatoabschnitte. Die c-Moll *Ciacona* (Nr. 2) ist sowohl an Figurierung als auch an Harmonien reich, und es ist bemerkenswert, dass das eigentliche Thema nach Takt 41 fast ganz aufgegeben wird, und nur sein harmonisches Grundgerüst beibehalten wird. Elemente, die für Buxtehude typisch sind, wie z.B. die rhetorischen Pausen gegen Ende des Stückes und die Sechzehntelfiguration ab Takt 53, stehen neben Kompositionstechniken, die aus anderen deutschen Klavierchaconnen, wie denen von Johann Caspar Kerll oder Johann Pachelbel bekannt sind. Zu diesen gehören punktierte Rhythmen und der arpeggierte oder *séparé*-Stil.

Die wichtigsten Änderungen und Entwicklungen in der norddeutschen Orgelmusik des späten 17. Jahrhunderts fanden im Gebiet des *Praeludiums* statt. Diese Tatsache spiegelt das zunehmende Interesse an der Orgelmusik ausserhalb der unmittelbaren Erfordernisse des Gottesdienstes. Im Gegensatz zum Schema 'Präludium und Fuge', das in Bachs reifen Orgelwerken häufig vorkommt, war die Struktur des frühen *Praeludiums* keineswegs einheitlich. Als Modell zur Struktur diente die italienische Variationskanzone, in der mehrere fugale Abschnitte über Varianten des gleichen Themas oft durch kurze freie Abschnitte verbunden wurden. Nicolaus Bruhns (1665–1697) hatte als junger Mann das Glück, bei Buxtehude, dem führenden Vertreter des *Praeludiums* (siehe Band 11, Nr. 7), zu studieren, und der Fanfarenstoss auf dem Pedal am Anfang seines *Praeludiums* (Nr. 4) gehörte wahrscheinlich zu den Kompositionstechniken, die er von seinem Lehrer übernahm. Obwohl dieses Werk nur einen einzigen Fugenabschnitt enthält, sind Spuren der Variationskanzone in der mehrteiligen Struktur und in der thematischen Beziehung zwischen der Fuge und dem im Takt 89 beginnenden *Allegro* deutlich erkennbar. Das Hauptthema der Fuge hat eine bemerkenswerte Ähnlichkeit mit dem Thema von Corelli (aus seinen Triosonaten Op. 3 aus dem Jahre 1689), das J. S. Bach in seiner h-Moll Fuge BWV579 benutzte, und die Tatsache, dass Bruhns nicht nur Organist sondern auch Geigenvirtuose war, erklärt einigermassen seine Vertrautheit mit dem italienischen Streicherstil.

Auch das *Praeludium con Fuga* (Nr. 6) von Böhm zeigt in der Sechzehntelfiguration und in der sequenzierenden Harmonie, welche die Fuge von Takt 53 an dominiert, seine Kenntnisse der zeitgenössischen italienischen Streichmusik. Die wiederholten Töne und die Pausen im Hauptthema der Fuge sind für den norddeutschen Stil des späten 17. Jahrhunderts typisch, aber in seiner Gesamtstruktur ist das Werk eines der ersten Zeugnisse für die Entwicklung in Richtung der zweiteiligen Präludien und Fugen des 18. Jahrhunderts.

---

1 Siehe M. Seiffert; 'Matthias Weckmann und das Collegium Musicum in Hamburg', *Sammelbände der internationalen Musik-Gesellschaft*, ii (1900–1901), S. 76

Ornamentierung

Während des späteren 17. Jahrhunderts wurde der in Band 10 und 11 dieser Sammlung beschriebene Ornamentierungsstil, d.h. im Grunde genommen der Renaissancestil, von dem für die französischen *clavecinistes* typischen Barockstil abgelöst. Die wesentlichen neuen Elemente dieses Stils waren der zunehmende Gebrauch des Vorschlags, sowohl allein als auch vor Trillern und Mordenten, und eine gewisse rhythmische Flexibilität bei der Ausführung von Ornamenten.

Böhms *Vater unser* (Nr. 5) ist eines der kunstvollsten Beispiele für den Gebrauch des neuen Stils unter den deutschen Organisten an der Wende des 18. Jahrhunderts, und stellt ziemliche Anforderungen an den Ausführenden. Die Begleitung sorgt für einen regelmässigen rhythmischen Puls, während die *cantus firmus*-Stimme erhebliche Freiheit des Ausdrucks benötigt, besonders wo zusätzliche kleine Noten gesetzt sind. Das Zeichen ⁓ bedeutet ein *tremblement*, einen auf der oberen Nebennote beginnenden Triller, bei dem die Anzahl der Reperkussionen je nach Zusammenhang verschieden ist. An Stellen, wo der Beginn auf dem oberen Ton die Melodieführung stört (z.B. Takte 31–33) ist ein *tremblement lié* vorzuziehen, bei dem die obere Nebennote

an die vorhergehende Melodienote gebunden ist. Das Zeichen ⁓ bedeutet den *pincé* oder Mordent, einen schnellen Wechsel zwischen dem Hauptton und der unteren Nebennote. Der Schleifer wird durch das Zeichen ⁓ angegeben. Laut der Beschreibungen in französischen Lehrbüchern beginnt dieser auf dem Schlag ⁓ , aber einige deutsche Quellen[2] deuten auf die Ausführung vor dem Schlag hin. Die kleinen Verzierungsnoten gehören wahrscheinlich in den Takten 16, 28 und 36 vor den Schlag, aber in den Takten 5 und 10, wo sie nach einer Pause auftreten, passen sie vielleicht besser auf den Schlag.

Die anderen Stücke in dem vorliegenden Band enthalten keine Ornamentierungszeichen, aber dem erfahrenen Spieler steht es wie beim früheren Repertoire frei, nach Belieben Verzierungen mit Diskretion und in einem angemessenen Stil hinzuzufügen.

2 z.B. J. G. Walther: *Praecepta der musicalischen Composition* (Leipzig, 1708), und eine Bearbeitung von Bruhns von *Nun komm, der Heiden Heiland*, in welcher die Schleifer vor dem Schlag voll ausgeschrieben sind.

Registrierung

Viele der norddeutschen Orgeln, die während des 17. Jahrhunderts gebaut oder vergrössert wurden, waren von erheblicher Grösse und boten zahllose Möglichkeiten für die Solo- und Begleitungskombinationen, die zur Aufführung von Choralbearbeitungen notwendig waren, und ausserdem eine Anzahl von *pleni* zur Aufführung von freien Werken. Die Pedalwerke gehörten zu den grössten in ganz Europa. Es standen Buxtehude in der Lübecker Marienkirche zwei Orgeln zur Verfügung; die kleinere davon, die sogenannte 'Totentanzorgel' hatte drei Manuale und Pedalwerk, während die Orgel im Westbau zu Buxtehudes Zeit folgende Register hatte:[3]

Werk		*Rückpositiv*	
Principal	16′	Principal	8′
Quintadena	16′	Bordun	16′
Octava	8′	Blockflöte	8′
Spitz-Flöte	8′	Sesquialtera	II
Octava	4′	Hohl-Flöte	8′
Hohlflöte	4′	Quintadena	8′
Nasat	3′ [=2⅔′]	Octava	4′
Rauschpfeiffe	IV	Spiel-Flöte	2′
Scharff	IV	Mixtura	V
Mixtura	XV	Dulcian	16′
Trommete	16′	Baarpfeiffe	8′
Trommete	8′	Trichter-Regal	8′
Zinke	8′	Vox humana	8′
		Scharff	IV–V
Brust		*Pedal*	
Principal	8′	Principal	32′
Gedact	8′	Sub-Bass	16′
Octava	4′	Octava	8′
Hohlflöte	4′	Bauerflöte	2′
Sesquialtera	II	Mixtura	VI
Feld-Pfeiffe	2′	Gross-Posaun (ab F?)	32′
Gemshorn	2′	Posaune	16′
Sifflet	1½′	Trommete	8′
Mixtura	VIII	Principal	16′
Cimbel	III	Gedact	8′
Krumhorn	8′	Octava	4′
Regal	8′	Nachthorn	2′
		Dulcian	16′

'heibey ein Cimbel-Stern /		*(Pedal)*	
zwo Trummeln / zweene		Krumhorn	8′
Tremulanten'		Cornet	2′
[Koppelung]			

In einem Bericht über Matthias Weckmanns Vorspiel an der Hamburger Jacobikirche erzählt sein Schüler Johann Kortkamp,[4] dass Weckmann an einer Stelle eine von seinem ehemaligen Lehrer Jacob Praetorius bevorzugte Choralregistrierung benutzte, und zwar die folgende: Oberwerk: Trommete 8′, Zinke 8′, Nassat 2′, Gemsshorn 2′, Hohlfleute 4′; Rückpositiv: Prinzipal 8′, Octave 4′ (für die leiseren Mittelstimmen), Pedal: Posaune 16′, Trommete 8′ und 4′, Cornet 2′.[5] Hierbei ist folgendes bemerkenswert: die Benutzung von Soloregistern sowohl im Oberwerk wie auch im Pedalwerk, die besondere Kombination von Zungen-, Flöten-und Aliquotstimmen im Oberwerk, und die aussergewöhnliche Benutzung des Rückpositivs für die Begleitstimmen. Eine derartige Kombination könnte sich für die 2. Strophe von Weckmanns *Gelobet seist du, Jesu Christ* (Nr. 1) eignen, wo die Choralmelodie sowohl in der Oberstimme als auch in dem Pedal erscheint. Die Angaben über die Manuale in der Quelle deuten aber darauf hin, dass die Rollen des Rückpositivs und des Oberwerks vertauscht werden sollten, damit das Rückpositiv wie gewöhnlich die Melodie trägt.

Die Angaben zur Registrierung, die Böhm am Anfang seines *Vater unser im Himmelreich* (Nr. 5) machte, deuten etwa hin auf Prinzipalton im Pedalwerk, Flöten im Oberwerk und Soloregister im Rückpositiv: wahrscheinlich entweder eine Solozungenstimme wie z.B. Regal oder Krummhorn oder eine Sesquialtera-Kombination.

Es gibt nur wenige Anhaltspunkte zur Registrierung von Werken im freien Stil, aber angesichts ihrer unterteilten Struktur und der komplizierten Manualwechsel, die bei manchen Choralsätzen angegeben sind, ist es wahrscheinlich, dass Manualwechsel zwischen den Abschnitten angebracht sind.

Geoffrey Webber
Oxford, 1987

3 Aus F. E. Niedt: *Musicalische Handleitung* (Hamburg, 1721; Nachdruck von Frits Knuf B.V.: die Niederlande, 1976), S. 189

4 Siehe J. T. Kite-Powell: *The Visby (Petri) Organ Tablature: Investigation and Critical Edition*, Quellen-Kataloge zur Musikgeschichte, xiv (Wilhelmshaven: Heinrichshofen, 1979)

5 Der Bauplan der Orgel in der Jacobikirche steht in Band 11.

Böhm: Praeludium con Fuga
(Staatsbibliothek Preussischer Kulturbesitz,
Mus. ms. 30381, p. 41)

1. *Gelobet seist du, Jesu Christ*

MATTHIAS WECKMANN *(c1619–1674)*

15th-century/Wittenberg, 1524

Ge - lo - bet seist du, Je - su Christ, dass du Mensch ge - wor - den bist von ei - ner Jung - frau, das ist wahr, des freu - et sich der En - gel Schar. Ky - ri - e - leis.

(Luther)

Primus Versus

[Ped.]

Secundus Versus
Auff 2 Clavir
Rucp[ositiv]

Org.*

Org.

Pedal

*Org[el] = Hauptwerk.

4

Tertius Versus
Auff 2 Clavir a 4

Quartus Versus a 3

Pedal

2. *Ciacona*

DIETRICH BUXTEHUDE *(c1637–1707)*

Manual

Pedale

Pedal

[Manual]

[Ped.]

[Ped.]

*Interpretation: *etc.*

3. *Mensch, willt du leben seliglich*

DIETRICH BUXTEHUDE *(c1637–1707)*

Wittenberg, 1524

Mensch, willt du le-ben se-lig-lich und bei Gott blei-ben e — — — wig-lich,

sollt du hal-ten die zehn Ge-bot, die uns ge-beut __ un-ser Gott. __ Ky-ri-e-leis.

(Luther)

4. *Praeludium*

NICOLAUS BRUHNS *(1665–1697)*

5. *Vater unser im Himmelreich*

à 2 Clav. et Pedal

GEORG BÖHM *(1661–1733)*

Leipzig, 1539

Va - ter un - ser im Him - mel - reich, der du uns al - le heis - sest gleich

Brü - der sein und dich ru - fen an und willst das Be - ten von uns han

gab, dass nicht bet al - lein der Mund, hilf, dass es geh von Her - zens - grund.

(Luther)

Rückpos.

Oberwerk Piano

Pedal Forte

6. *Praeludium con Fuga*

GEORG BÖHM *(1661–1733)*

Ped.

Ped.   Ped.

Critical Commentary

Sources are listed for each piece, together with original titles and/or ascriptions where present. Where there is more than one source, the first listed represents the main source for the edition (see Editorial Procedure, §7); any deviations from the main source are detailed in the commentary below.

The following RISM sigla are used to indicate the libraries in which manuscripts are located:

D–B   – Berlin, Staatsbibliothek Preussischer Kulturbesitz
D–Bds   – Berlin, Deutsche Staatsbibliothek
D-LEm – Leipzig, Musikbibliothek der Stadt
D-Lr   – Lüneburg, Ratsbücherei
NL-DHgm – The Hague, Gemeentemuseum

The following abbreviations are used:

S   – soprano
A   – alto
T   – tenor
B   – bass
lh   – left hand
rh   – right hand

Pitches are notated as follows:

C′–B′ C–B   c–b   c′–b′ c″–b″ c‴–b‴

32 T 7-9 ♩♫ means that in bar 32 the seventh, eighth and ninth notes of the tenor part are a crotchet and two quavers in the source; 4 rh middle voice 2,3 f′♯ g′♯ means that in bar 4, right hand, middle voice, the second and third notes are middle octave F♯ and G♯ in the source.

1. **Gelobet seist du, Jesu Christ**
   D-Lr KN 207/21. *Gelobet seystu / Jesu Christ: á 4. / Primus Versus MWM*
   15 A 3 g′ / 18 S 8 f′ / 44 B 4–5 ♫ / 104 A 6 d′ / 114 direction *Org.* is on 1st beat

2. **Ciacona** (BuxWV159)
   D–LEm Ms. III.8.4. ('Andreas-Bach-Buch'), f. 33v–35r. *Ciaconne di Diet. Buxtehude*
   57 S 9–12 d″e″bd″c″

3. **Mensch, willt du leben seliglich** (BuxWV206)
   NL-DHgm Mus. Ms. 4 G.14, p. 96. *Mensch wiltu leben seeliglich. D.B.*
   9 A 7–8 ♫

4. **Praeludium**
   D–Bds Mus. ms. 40294/4. *Praeludium ex E di N Bruhns*
   Continuous barlines reflect the use of vertical strokes in the source.
   10 A 2 ♩ / 20 lh 1 a′ / 32 A 1 e′ / 37 S 12 d′ / 52 S l d″ / 107 S 2 g″

5. **Vater unser im Himmelreich**
   D–B Mus. ms. Bach P802, f. 90. *Vater unser im Himmelreich / a 2 clav. et Pedal / di Böhm*
   The small notes in the rh seem to have been added to the MS at a later stage.
   24 rh no ♭ to b′s

6. **Praeludium con Fuga**
   D–B Mus. ms. 30381, No. 7, pp. 41–3. [On separate title-page:] *Praeludium con Fuga ex A♭. / Pedaliter. / di / Monsieur Böhm*
   35 A 3 a″

Appendix
Analytical Index to the Faber Early Organ Series

Within each formal category, works are listed in approximately chronological order. Each title is followed by the relevant volume number (roman type) and the number of the work within the volume (italic type).

1. Mass Movements

Anon. (published 1531 by Attaingnant): *Sanctus and Benedictus* 7/1

Hans Buchner (1483–1538): *Sanctus trium regium* 13/14; *Kyrie festivum primum* 13/15

John Redford (d.1547): *Agnus Dei* 1/3

Hieronymus Praetorius (1560–1629): *Kyrie Martyrum* 11/1

Adriano Banchieri (1568–1634): *Gloria in excelsis* 17/10; *Prima toccata del terzo tuono autentico alla levatione del Santissimo Sacramento* 17/11; *Secondo dialogo* 17/12

Girolamo Frescobaldi (1583–1643): *Toccata avanti la Messa della Domenica* 17/13a; *Kyrie della Domenica* 17/13b; *Toccata per le levatione* 17/13c; *Canzona post il comune* 17/13d

Giovanni Salvatore (d.?1688): *Versi sopra il Kyrie* 18/5

Johann Jacob Froberger (1616–1667): *Toccata da sonarsi alla levatione* 14/12

Alessandro Poglietti (d.1683): *Toccatina per l'introito* 15/2

Abraham van den Kerckhoven (c.1618–1701): *Kyrie-Christe-Kyrie* 10/6

Nicolas Gigault (c.1627–1707): *Kyrie double à 5 parties* 8/11; *Fugue grave recherchée sur le Kyrie à 4* 8/12

André Raison (c.1645–1719): *Kyrie* 8/13; *Élévation en C bémol* 8/14

François Couperin (1668–1733): Three movements from *Messe à l'usage ordinaire des paroisses* 9/2a–c; Two movements from *Messe pour les convents* 9/3a–b

Nicolas de Grigny (1672–1703): *Récit de Tierce en taille* 9/6a; *Dialogue pour la Communion* 9/6b; *Deo gratias* 9/6c

Gaspard Corrette (d. before 1733): Three movements from *Messe du 8ᵉ ton* 9/8a–c

2. Magnificat Settings

Anon. (published 1531 by Attaingnant): *Magnificat quarti toni* 7/2

Anon. (?John Redford, d.1547): *Magnificat* 1/2

Antonio de Cabezón (1510–1566): *Versos del 8° tono de Magnificat* 4/13

Girolamo Cavazzoni (c.1525–after 1577): *Magnificat quarti toni* 16/4

Anon. (?French, 1617): *Magnificat secundi toni* 7/4

Jehan Titelouze (1562/3–1633): *Magnificat quinti toni (three versets)* 7/6

Jacob Praetorius (1586–1651): *Magnificat secundi toni (verse 2)* 11/2

Johann Erasmus Kindermann (1616–1655): *Magnificat octavi toni* 14/10

Johann Pachelbel (1653–1706): *Magnificat septimi toni (four versets)* 15/11

Jean-Adam Guilain (fl.1702–1739): *Dialogue du 2ᵉ ton* 9/5a; *Petit Plein jeu* 9/5b

3. Other Latin *Cantus firmus* Settings

Arnolt Schlick (c.1460–after 1521): *Da pacem* 13/1

Hans Buchner (1483–1538): *Puer natus est* 13/16

John Redford (d.1547): *O quam glorifica* 1/4

Thomas Preston (fl. mid-16th century): *Felix namque* 1/5; *Benedictus sit Deus Pater* 1/6

Thomas Tallis (c.1505–?1585): *Alleluia: Per te Dei Genitrix* 1/8; *Ecce tempus idoneum* 1/9

Juan Bermudo (c.1510–?1565): *Veni creator spiritus* 4/4; *Pange lingua* 4/5

Antonio de Cabezón (1510–1566): *Beata viscera Mariae virginis* 4/12

William Blitheman (c.1525–1591): *Gloria tibi Trinitas* 1/11

Girolamo Cavazzoni (c.1525–after 1577): *Christe Redemptor omnium* 16/3

Rocco Rodio (c.1535–after 1615): *Ave maris stella* 16/5

William Byrd (c.1543–1623): *Clarifica me Pater* 1/12

Simon Lohet (before c.1550–1611): *Media vita in morte* 14/3

Jehan Titelouze (1562/3–1633): *Ad coenam Agni providi* 7/5

John Bull (c.1563–1628): *Gloria tibi Trinitas* 2/6

Samuel Scheidt (1587–1654): *Christe qui lux es et dies* 10/7

Giovanni Battista Fasolo (c.1600–after 1659): *Hinno per la Ascensione del terzo tono: Jesu nostra redemptio* 18/7

?Gaspar dos Reis (d.1674): *Concertado No. 3 sobre Ave maris stella* 5/6

Pablo Bruna (1611–1679): *Pange lingua, 5° tono* 6/3; *Otra pange lingua, 5° tono* 6/4

Anon. (French, c.1650): *Ave maris stella* 7/9

Guillaume-Gabriel Nivers (c.1632–1714): *Ave maris stella* 8/7

Juan Cabanilles (1644–1712): *Pange lingua* 6/9

Nicolas de Grigny (1672–1703): *Pange lingua, en taille à 4* 9/7

4. Miscellaneous Liturgical Versets

Manuel Rodrigues Coelho (c.1555–1635): *Versos do 3° tom* 4/15

Antonio Valente (fl.1565–1580): *Versi sopra il re* 16/6

Fr. Martinho García de Olague (17th century): *Fabordão e versos do 1° tom* 5/8

?Gaspar dos Reis (d.1674): *Tenção sobre o 5° Kyrie* 5/7

Alessandro Poglietti (d.1683): *Praeludia, Cadenzen und Fugen* 15/1

Louis Couperin (1626–1661): *Fantaisie* 8/1; *Duo* 8/2

Nicolas Lebègue (1631–1702): *Cromhorne ou Tierce en taille* 8/8a; *Trio à 3 claviers* 8/8b; *Dessus de Cromhorne ou de Trompette* 8/8c; *Offertoire en C* 8/9

Jean-Henri d'Anglebert (1635–1691): *Fugue grave* 8/5; *Quatuor sur le Kyrie* 8/6

Gilles Jullien (c.1650/53–1703): *Dessus de Voix humaine* 8/15; *Basse de Trompette* 8/16

Jacques Boyvin (1649–1706): *Suite du 5ᵉ ton* 9/1

Louis Marchand (1669–1732): *Basse de Trompette* 9/4

Louis-Nicolas Clérambault (1676–1749): *Récits de Cromhorne, et de Cornet séparé, en dialogue* 9/9a; *Dialogue sur les Grands jeux* 9/9b

Franz Xaver Murschhauser (1683–1738): *Praeambulum octavi toni, five Fugues & Finale* 15/6

5. Vernacular *Cantus firmus* Settings

Arnolt Schlick (c.1460–1521): *Maria zart* 13/3

Hans Kotter (c.1485–1541): *Aus tiefer Not* 13/13

Simon Lohet (before c.1550–1611): *Nun welche hie ihr Hoffnung gar* 14/1

Henderick Speuy (c.1575–1625): *Duo van den Psalm 24* 10/3

Anthoni van Noordt (d.1675): *Psalm 24* 10/5

Heinrich Scheidemann (c.1585–1663): *Vater unser im Himmelreich* 11/4

Franz Tunder (c.1614–1667): *Komm, heiliger Geist, Herre Gott* 11/5

Johann Erasmus Kindermann (1616–1655): *Fuga super Ach wie sehnlich* 14/7; *Drifache Fuga super Christ lag in Todesbanden; Christus der selig macht; Da Jesus an dem Creuze stundt* 14/9

Matthias Weckmann (c.1619–1674): *Gelobet seist du, Jesu Christ* 12/1

Dietrich Buxtehude (c.1637–1707): *Ich ruf zu dir, Herr Jesu Christ* 11/6; *Mensch, willt du leben seliglich* 12/3

Johann Pachelbel (1653–1706): *Wie schön leuchtet der Morgenstern* 15/7; *Wir glauben all an einen Gott* 15/8

Georg Böhm (1661–1733): *Vater unser im Himmelreich* 12/5

6. Motet Intabulations

Anon. (published 1531 by Attaingnant): *Parce Domine* 7/3

Bernhard Schmid the elder (1535–1592): *Sicut mater consolatur* 13/18

7. Secular Intabulations

Arnolt Schlick (c.1460–after 1521): *Hoe losteleck* 13/2

Andrea Antico (c.1480–after 1539): *Chi non crede* 16/1

Marc'Antonio Cavazzoni (c.1490–c.1560): *L'autre jour par un matin* 16/2

Bernhard Schmid the elder (1535–1592): *Ein guter Wein ist lobenswerdt* 13/17

8. Preludes, Toccatas etc.

Leonhard Kleber (c.1495–1556): Three *Praeambula* 13/5, 7, 8; *Finale* 13/6

Hans Kotter (c.1485–1541): *Proemium in re* 13/9; *Preludium in fa* 13/10; *Fantasia in ut* 13/11; *Proemium in re* 13/12

Tomás de Santa María (d.?1570): *Del modo de tañer a corcheas* 4/8

Andrea Gabrieli (1510–1586): *Intonazione del sesto tono* 16/8

Claudio Merulo (1533–1604): *Toccata quarta del secondo tuono* 16/10

Luzzascho Luzzaschi (?1545–1607): *Toccata del quarto tuono* 16/11

Ercole Pasquini (d.1608/19): *Toccata* 17/1

Giovanni de Macque (?1548/50–1614): *Seconde stravaganze* 17/4

Jan Pieterszoon Sweelinck (1562–1621): *Toccata secundi toni* 10/1

Ascanio Mayone (c.1565–1627): *Toccata quarta* 17/4

William Brown (?d.1637): *Toccata* 2/7

Giovanni Maria Trabaci (c.1575–1647): *Toccata prima à quattro* 17/6

Girolamo Frescobaldi (1583–1634): *Toccata sesta per l'organo sopra i pedali, e senza* 18/1

Christian Michael (c.1593–1637): *Toccata 2* 14/4

Heinrich Scheidemann (c.1595–1663): *Praeambulum* 11/3

Michelangelo Rossi (1601/2–1656): *Toccata prima* 18/3

Johann Erasmus Kindermann (1616–1655): *Praeambulum 1 & 2 toni* 14/6; *Praeambulum 9 & 10 toni* 14/8

Johann Jacob Froberger (1616–1667): *Toccata* 14/11

Henry du Mont (1616–1684): *Prélude* 8/3; *Allemande* 8/4

Giovanni Salvatore (d.?1688): *Toccata seconda del nono tuono naturale* 18/4

Pedro de Araújo (late 17th century): *Obra de passo solto 8° tom* 5/10

Anon. (Spanish, 17th century): *Obra de falsas cromáticas de 1° tono* 6/6

Johann Kaspar Kerll (1627–1693): *Toccata IV cromatica con durezze, e ligature* 15/4; *Toccata* 15/5

Nicolas Lebègue (c.1631–1702): *Une Vierge pucelle* 8/10

Dietrich Buxtehude (c.1637–1707): *Praeludium* in A minor 11/7; *Ciacona* in C minor 12/2

Bernardo Pasquini (1637–1710): *Toccata* 18/10

John Blow (1649–1708): *Voluntary in C* 3/4

Georg Muffat (1653–1704): *Toccata decima* 15/12; *Ciacona* 15/13

Henry Purcell (1659–1695): *Voluntary in G* 3/8

Anon. (?Blow and Purcell): *Trumpet Voluntary in D* 3/6

Georg Böhm (1661–1733): *Praeludium con Fuga in A minor* 12/6

Nicolaus Bruhns (1665–1697): *Praeludium* in E minor 12/4

9. Fantasias, Ricercares, Fugues etc.

Paul Hofhaimer (1459–1537): *Carmen* 13/4

Anon. (English, c.1530): *Two Early Sixteenth-century Pieces* 1/1

Heliadorus de Paiva (c.1500–1552): *Tento do 3° tom* 4/2; *Tento do 4° tom* 4/3

Anon. (English, ?mid-16th century): *Voluntary in Three Parts* 1/7

António de Cabezón (1510–1566): *Tiento sobre Cum sancto spiritu* 4/14

Andrea Gabrieli (1510–1586): *Ricercar del settimo tono* 16/9

William Blitheman (c.1525–1591): *Three Parts* 1/10

António Carreira (c.1525–c.1589): *Tento do 8° tom* 4/1

Spirindio Bertoldo (c.1530–1570): *Ricercar del sesto tuono* 16/7

Anon. (Spanish, 1557): *Tiento de 5° tono* 4/6

Tomás de Santa María (d.?1570): Three *Fugas* (canons) 4/9–11

Francisco Fernández Palero (d.1597): *Tiento de 7° tono super Philomena* 4/7

William Byrd (c.1543–1623): *A Fancy* 2/1

Simon Lohet (before c.1550–1611): *Decima Fuga* 14/2

Girolamo Diruta (c.1554–ater 1610): *Ricecare del settimo tuono* 17/9

Manuel Rodrigues Coelho (c.1555–1635): *Tento do 2° tom* 4/16

Sebastián Aguilera de Heredia (1561–1627): *Tiento de 4° tono de falsas* 5/4; *Registo baixo do 1° tom* 5/5

Jan Pieterszoon Sweelinck (1562–1621): *Fantasia* 10/2

Ascanio Mayone (c.1565–1627): *Ricercar primo* 17/3

Giovanni Paolo Cima (c.1570–after 1622): *Canzon quarta: La Pace* 17/7; *Ricercare à quattro* 17/8

Pieter Cornet (c.1570/80–1633): *Fantasia* 10/4

Thomas Weelkes (c.1575–1623): *Two Voluntaries* 2/2

Giovanni Maria Trabaci (c.1575–1647): *Canzona franzesa settima cromatica* 17/5

Orlando Gibbons (1583–1625): *A Fancy in C fa ut* 2/3; *A Fancy in Gamut flatt* 2/4; *A Short Preludio of Four Parts* 2/5

Vincenzo Pellegrini (d.1631/2): *Canzon detta la Capricciosa* 16/12

Girolamo Frescobaldi (1583–1643): *Recercar sesto sopra fa, fa, sol, la, fa* 18/2

Benjamin Cosyn (c.1570–c.1652): *Voluntary* 2/8

Anon. (English, early 17th century): *Two Voluntaries* 2/9

Thomas Tomkins (1572–1656): *Verse* 2/10; *A Fantasy* 2/11

Francisco Correa de Arauxo (c.1575–1654): *Tiento de 5° tono* 5/1; *Tiento de medio registro de baxon de 1° tono* 5/2; *Tiento de medio registro de dos tiples de 2° tono* 5/3

Johann Klemm (c.1595–after 1651): *Fuga XVIII à 3* 14/5

Richard Portman (d. c.1655): *Verse for Double Organ* 2/12

Charles Racquet (1597–1664): *Fantaisie* 7/7

Giovanni Battista Fasolo (c.1600–after 1659): *Canzon quarta del quarto tono naturale* 18/6

Luigi Battiferri (1600/10–after 1681): *Ricercare nono con tre soggetti* 18/8

Pablo Bruna (1611–1679): *Tiento de 1° tono de mano derecha* 6/1; *Tiento de falsas de 2° tono* 6/2

Anon. (Spanish, 17th century): *Obra de 8° tono, medio registro, mano izquierda* 6/5

Christopher Gibbons (1615–1676): *Voluntary in A minor for Double Organ* 3/1

Johann Jacob Froberger (1616–1667): *Fantasia sopra sol la re* 14/13; *Capriccio* 14/14

Alessandro Poglietti (d.1683): *Ricercar primi toni* 15/3

Matthew Locke (c.1622–1677): *Voluntary in A minor* 3/2; *Voluntary in A minor (from* Melothesia*)* 3/3

François Roberday (1624–1680): *Fugue et Caprice No. 3* 7/8

Pedro de Araújo (late 17th century): *Obra de 6° tom* 5/9

Juan Cabanilles (1644–1712): *Tiento de 4° tono lleno* 6/7; *Tiento de falsas de 4° tono* 6/8; *Tiento de batalla de 8° tono* 6/10

John Blow (1649–1708): *Cornet Voluntary in A minor* 3/5

Anon. (?John Blow): *Verse in G minor* 3/9

Johann Pachelbel (1653–1706): *Two fugues* 15/9–10

Henry Purcell (1659–1695): *Voluntary in D minor for Double Organ* 3/7

Ziani (late 17th century): *Capriccio* 18/9

William Croft (1678–1727): *Voluntary in A minor for Double Organ* 3/10; *Voluntary in D minor* 3/11

(1054/88) Hobbs the Printers of Southampton